CARS, CARS, CARS

# SILLY CARS

## by Melissa Abramovitz

Gail Saunders-Smith, PhD, Consulting Editor

Consultant: Leslie Mark Kendall, Curator
Petersen Automotive Museum
Los Angeles, California

CAPSTONE PRESS
a capstone imprint

Pebble Plus is published by Capstone Press,
1710 Roe Crest Drive, North Mankato, Minnesota 56003.
www.capstonepub.com

**Library of Congress Cataloging-in-Publication Data**
Abramovitz, Melissa, 1954–
  Silly cars / by Melissa Abramovitz.
      p. cm.—(Pebble plus. Cars, cars, cars)
  Summary: "Simple text and color photographs describe nine silly cars"—Provided by the publisher.
  Audience: K-3.
  Includes bibliographical references and index.
  ISBN 978-1-62065-089-9 (library binding)
  ISBN 978-1-62065-877-2 (paperback)
  ISBN 978-1-4765-1076-7 (eBook PDF)
  1.  Automobiles—Juvenile literature. 2.  Automobiles—Customizing—Juvenile literature.  I. Title. II. Series: Pebble plus.
Cars, cars, cars.
  TL147.A28 2013
  629.222—dc23                                                                                  2012031833

**Editorial Credits**
Erika L. Shores, editor; Kyle Grenz, designer; Laura Manthe, production specialist

**Photo Credits**
AP Images: James A. Finley, 19, The State News, Amanda McCoy, cover (left); Newscom: KRT, 9, Tass Photos/Vasily
Klyashko Itar, 15, WENN Photos/ZOB/CB2, 5, Newscom/ZUMA Press/Keystone Canada/Ken Stewart, cover (lower right),
11; Photo Courtesy of Ed Moore/Bellingham Auto Sales, 13; Shutterstock: Michael Stokes, 7, Telephone Car by Howard Davis
photo (c) Harrod Blank www.artcaragency.com, 21; The Golden Mean Kyrsten Mate & Jon Sarriugarte 2008
www.snailartcar.com, cover (upper right), 17

**Artistic Effects**
Shutterstock: 1xpert

## Note to Parents and Teachers

The Cars, Cars, Cars set supports national science standards related to science, technology,
and society. This book describes and illustrates silly cars. The images support early readers in
understanding the text. The repetition of words and phrases helps early readers learn new words.
This book also introduces early readers to subject-specific vocabulary words, which are defined in
the Glossary section. Early readers may need assistance to read some words and to use the Table of
Contents, Glossary, Read More, Internet Sites, and Index sections of the book.

Printed in the United States of America in North Mankato, Minnesota.
092012      006933CGS13

# Table of Contents

# Silly Cars

A bowling pin car? A hot dog car?

Some cars go that extra mile

to get a smile.

The Rinspeed Splash drives,

swims, and flies.

Hydrofoil wings lift it 2 feet

(0.6 meter) above water.

hydrofoil wing

The 2004 Rinspeed Splash is a sports car developed by Rinspeed Design.

A "funny car" is a type of race car.

Funny cars are super fast!

Top speeds can reach 330 miles

(531 kilometers) per hour.

**Funny cars are custom made from many types of car bodies.**

Wienermobiles have advertised

Oscar Mayer hot dogs since 1936.

Drivers are called "hotdoggers."

Wienermobile horns play

the Oscar Mayer hot dog song.

**Wienermobiles are built on various car and truck frames.**

# Sillier Cars

Which way are you going?

Push-me-pull-you cars have

two front ends.

Some of these cars can drive

forward from either end.

COMING OR GOING

**Push-me-pull-you cars are made by welding together two half-cars of any kind.**

Sir Vival is a safe but odd-looking car. Rubber bumpers, padding, and two sections help keep passengers safe.

**Sir Vival is a custom car built from a 1948 Hudson.**

Vasily Lazarenko's wood car is

split down the middle.

Only one side has a roof.

**The wood car was built with a 1981 Opel engine and frame.**

# Silliest Cars

The Golden Mean is

a glow-in-the-dark snail car.

Flames shoot from the feelers!

The car is a work of art

on wheels.

**Jon Sarriugarte built The Golden Mean from a 1966 Volkswagen Beetle.**

Bowling-lanes owner Mike Skrovan built a wood and steel bowling pin car. It's the world's largest bowling pin.

The bowling pin car was built using a 1936 Studebaker frame.

The Phone Car advertises
Datel phones. A driver sees
through a tinted window that
holds the buttons. The horn rings
like a phone.

**Howard Davis built the Phone Car on a 1975 Volkswagen Beetle frame.**

# Glossary

**advertise**—to give information about something you want to sell

**custom made**—built for a certain reason

**hydrofoil wing**—one of two V-shaped parts that let the Rinspeed Splash ride above the water

**passenger**—someone besides the driver who rides in a vehicle

# Read More

**Adamson, Thomas K.** *Hot Rods.* Rev It Up! North Mankato, Minn.: Capstone Press, 2011.

**Clark, Willow**. *Cars on the Move.* Transportation Station. New York: PowerKids Press, 2010.

**Doman, Mary Kate**. *Cool Cars.* All about Big Machines. Berkeley Heights, N.J.: Enslow Elementary, 2012.

# Internet Sites

FactHound offers a safe, fun way to find Internet sites related to this book. All of the sites on FactHound have been researched by our staff.

Here's all you do:

Visit *www.facthound.com*

Type in this code: 9781620650899

Super-cool stuff!

Check out projects, games and lots more at
**www.capstonekids.com**

# Index

Word Count: 198
Grade: 1
Early-Intervention Level: 23